Molly's Story

by

MOLLY PARK

AS TOLD TO JUNE THISTLETHWAITE

Best Wishes

June

Thistlethwaite

Thyme Press

Other books by the author

Cumbrian Women Remember; Published 1995
reprinted 1995, 1997 & 1998

Cumbria The War Years; Published 1997

Cover photography by Keith Bales Photography, Workington

Published by Thyme Press, 5 Finley Close,
Kendal, Cumbria LA9 6DW
First Published 1998

Typeset by Indent Ltd, Kendal
Printed by Kent Valley Colour Printers, Kendal

British Library Cataloguing in Publication Data
A Catalogue of this book is available from the British Library
ISBN 0-9531695-3-7

Contents

Acknowledgements

I am grateful to Molly for telling me her story and supplying photographs to correspond. Many thanks to Tom Park and J. Wiggins for their time and patience in reading through the proofs of this story; John Akrigg, Molly's nephew, who introduced us and supplied other family photographs; Beacon Heritage Centre (Whitehaven) for allowing me to use the photograph on page 39 ; and to Quicksnaps (Kendal).

Introduction

Molly is a very special lady as she embodies most Cumbrian women of her generation. On reading of Molly's early life, living with her grandparents because there were so many children at home, people will say, 'Yes, that happened to my mother.' Recalling the hard times between the wars, again this will bring back memories. In most families there are women, who as girls, went into service or took menial jobs simply because they were told to. They had no choice. There are countless women who can recall their hard lives on farms, exhausted and living with the continual fear of bankruptcy hanging over them. Many others live with the heartbreaking memories of difficult pregnancies and babies who died. Others who brought up a child or children on their own, scrimping and saving as Molly did so that their family may have a better life.

However, this is not a story of gloom. Most of the events are recalled with a smile, a giggle and a dry sense of humour. There was Molly's father who more than eighty years ago threw away the cuvvins she was eating with the dire prediction she would die of food poisoning. Remembering a last week in service and training another maid who also didn't want to stay, Molly laughs now at her own alarm as she implored the maid, 'For the Lord's sake, let me out of here before you do go home.' Then there was the tale of the live cockerel kept in the post office locker. The reminiscences came thick and fast.

In common with most Cumbrian women, Molly has played down her achievements. She mentions that she worked at a post office for twenty seven years. Unfortunately she slides over the fact that she studied and passed all her post office examinations during this time. Considering Molly's circumstances, this was no little achievement and is a credit to her determination and ability.

This is the first book I've written where I've asked someone to write a foreword. Usually, this would be undertaken by someone in the public eye. That wouldn't impress Molly. There could only be one person to write a foreword and that is Tom, Molly's son. His life is pivotal to *Molly's Story*.

Foreword

When June asked me to write a brief foreword to her collection of reminiscences for my mother's life, I knew it would be a difficult and emotional task. I am very proud of this independent, tough little lady. With the bare bones of her life exposed, it is easy to discern the reasons for mum's vulnerability. Stemming from her early life is the growth, through necessity, of her determination and self-reliance. She has had to rely on these strengths many times since.

Having lived through more than two-thirds of Mother's life I know first hand of the deep and savage hurts inflicted on her, not only by her marriage but also by the interventions of others without wit or knowledge to understand. Her ability to rise above these, and the many obstacles in her path is bedded deeply in her great love for me and her determination to ensure that I suffered as little as possible. I feel very humble indeed when I see the extent of her self-sacrifice and recognise what it has cost her. I owe her a far greater debt than can ever be repaid.

Needless to say Gran still lives alone, the sole survivor of her generation. She is content with little, still knitting squares for blankets for 'old people', and having given away much of her clothing, bedding etc. to various disaster appeals. Her life is lived through my wife and I, our daughters and their husbands and, best of all, her great, grandchildren. In her words she has 'coped' with life. I am pleased that her descendants will now be able to judge for themselves just how much an understatement this is.

TP 30/8/98

ONE

Standing, Molly is on the left and Blanche on the right.
Front, the twins, Blanche and George. 1910

A year and a week old

The midwife at Hensingham was old Mrs Patterson. When I was being born, she couldn't manage to deliver me and sent for Dr Muriel. Years later, Mrs Patterson told me that I'd been a breech baby and bleeding from the nose and ears. Dr Muriel had looked at me, shook his head and said, 'It'll do no good.' But Mrs Patterson picked me up, rolled me in a blanket and took me to her house where Mr Patterson was sitting in front of a big fire. She turned to her husband and said, 'Andrew, I'm going to bath this baby, clean her up and then thou can sit and nurse her.'

Well, they made a bottle up for me with Robertson's patent barley and I managed to suck that. So Andrew sat up all night in front of the fire nursing me and his wife relieved him from time to time. They kept me for a few days until they knew I was all right before taking me back to my mother. 'I think we willed you to live' said Mrs Patterson.

That happened on 6th August 1908 at Beckbottoms, Ribton Moorside at Hensingham. My mother already had two children. There had been William who died in infancy; eleven months later came Sally who was a year and nine months older than me; when I was a year and a week old, mother had twins, Blanche and George; Edna was born a year and five months after the twins and then came Katy, eleven months later; Raymond the youngest child arrived eleven years on. He eventually went to the Grammar School and was accepted for Cardiff University. His entrance fee and everything was paid for but he caught meningitis and died.

Anyway, when the twins George and Blanche were born, Mrs Patterson was called to the house and because Mother was very ill, Dr Muriel again was sent for. Now, Granda called at the house to see how his daughter was. He hadn't known the babies had been born and Mother was ill. When he saw the situation, he picked me up and took me back to Grandma at Goosebutts. I never went home to live again, until I was twelve and a half. It was very rare I went to see my own parents because they lived six and a half miles away and you had to go by 'shanks's pony'. There was the railway, two and a half miles away at Moor Row, which went to Whitehaven but there was never any money to go on that.

Grandma and Granda still had four of their family living at home. There was Aunt Kate, Aunt Ginny, Aunt Sally and Uncle Billy. Until I was a big girl, I thought of my grandparents as my mother and my daddy. The aunts and uncle in the house, were my older sisters and brother. To me, my real parents were 'our Mary, Jack Taylor and their bairns.'

Granda & Grandma with some of thir family and friends near Whitehaven. C. 1900
Grandma is back row standing centre. Granda is sitting 2nd left.
Their daughter, Mary (Molly's mother) is kneeling centre.
Front row, 3rd left is Auntie Kate.
1st & 2nd right is Auntie Sally & Uncle Billy.

Home to me at Goosebutts was a cottage with a wash-house, coal shed and water closet as it was known in them days. Most cottages had dry pettys and a pump or well but we had running water. Two taps, in fact. Inside the cottage was a black leaded fireplace, with two ovens, both with brass knobs. There was a steel fender, jockey bar and fire irons, a jack which let out to hang a pan on, one of those three legged iron pans with a lid and a handle like a kettle. Kettles and pans were black leaded weekly after soot was scraped off with a blunt knife. We had a brass rod under the mantle-shelf for airing clothes on. There was a wooden oval tub that Grandad made, painted green with black iron bands on. It had handles hewn out of wood. I had my nightly bath in this tub until I was big enough to put into the wooden dolly tub. Grandad made that too, and dolly legs for use on wash day. Irons were either flat irons made of iron or box irons with two iron heaters. These were put into the fire to get red hot and transferred to a box.

The cottage had two bedrooms. Granda and Uncle Billy slept in the back bedroom. In the front bedroom there were two mattresses on the bed. Every night a mattress was put on the floor and made up as a bed. Grandma, Auntie Katie and me slept in the big bed and Aunt Sally and Jinny slept on the floor on the shaky down.

From our bedroom window we viewed the mountains around Ennerdale Valley and in the green fields all around we could see Highland cattle grazing. Early in a morning, there would be Mr Bound's cockerel crowing and hens clucking. In spring, chicks would be cheeping, little lambs frisking and playing and the birdsong of the corncrake and pewit. Nearby were plantations where at night bats squeaked and flew low, owls hooted and rooks and crows nestled in the trees calling cra, cra. In our garden were the flowers. We used to have Canterbury bells, sweet williams, old fashioned English roses that smelled beautiful, proper tea roses and honeysuckle. In the window boxes were dwarf nasturtiums and lobelia. It was paradise.

TWO

A blinking lie!!

Goosebutts was a hamlet of twelve cottages with a big house. Then there was a mile of plantations with a crossroad and the Summergrove mansion in the middle of it. The mansion had two lodges, a front one and a back one. The big house belonged to the Spedding family but the Rotherys lived there. There were seven mansions in the parish, most of them lived in by industrialists. John Musgrove, he was the High Sheriff of Cumberland, lived at Holme Wood.

Now, there was a narrow lane between Musgrove's house and the land that belonged to another mansion. Well, we used to go up this narrow lane for a short cut and some boys had taken snowdrops from the wood. "Old Mussie" caught them, took the lads back to school, and gave them a lecture in front of everybody on thieving. Mind you, they'd only picked a few snowdrops and the woods were white with them.

Further on there were two old sandstone quarries full of water. Cumbrians used to call them freestone quarries and nearly all cottage floors were freestone. Then there was Galemire isolation hospital and after that was Moor Row. Most of the streets at Moor Row had Cornish names because years ago, that's where Cornish tin miners went to live. In the other direction was Mill Hill, where a family called Messenger had a farm and mill. They used to grind wheat and corn to make wheat flour and oat meal. Oh, it was lovely, the smell of oat meal being roasted. The river we called Mill Hill Beck, and when the miners used to wash ore, the water ran red.

Mrs Grant lived at Summer Grove front lodge but when she died, the school attendance officer, Mr Murphy and his daughter Margaret lived there. He was known as 'Father' Murphy, a term of endearment, by all the school children. Once a year when Mr Murphy went to a conference for a week, I stayed with Margaret at the lodge. She took me with her to the Roman Catholic Church at Cleator, to see a never to be forgotten procession and the opening of the Grotto. And one beautiful moonlit night, old Father Murphy pointed at the moon and said, 'See that Molly, that's Paddy's lantern. When you see a new moon, shake the pennies in your pocket and you won't be short of a penny' Now, that was a blinking lie!

THREE

They've starched me britches

I'll tell you what happened one day. I was at school and everybody was out of our house except Grandma. Somebody knocked on the door and so she shouted, 'Come in' and in walked young Father Clayton from Southern Ireland who had just come to Cleator and was looking up his parishioners. When Grandma saw him she said, 'I'm not of your faith, you know but we're all fighting for the same spot. Come in, me lad and ah'll mek thee a cup of tea.' So she made him a cup of tea and gave him a bit of cake and when he'd finished, Father Clayton said, 'Can I come again?' Oh, Grandma thought he was a smashing lad. He was, he was a real nice lad.

Now Father Clayton had come to the wrong house as he was looking for Esther who lived next door. Esther was from Southern Ireland and was married to a Billy, who was Scottish. At Cleator folk were Scottish or mostly Irish and that's why it was called Little Ireland. They used to say 'our wee' this and 'our wee' that. A child was always called 'a wee un'. When I eventually went back home to live at Whitehaven, they christened (called) me 'our wee-wee'. Nothing at all to do with the waterworks, just the fact that I always used to say 'wee this and that'.

I had to go to Sunday School at the Parish Church. Mind you, the only Sunday School trips we had at Keekle were to a farmer's barn where we had sandwiches and something to drink. When I was old enough I went to bible class in an afternoon and then six o'clock service at night. If we went to a cantata, instead of going to Sunday School, we had to walk in a procession and take something, even if it was only an egg for the hospital or church. Walking in the procession we had to sing, though half of us hadn't a pennyworth of tune between us. But we thought we did well and sang –

They've starched me britches

Dropping, dropping, dropping
Hear the pennies fall
Every one for Jesus
He shall have them all.
If we have not money
we can give him love
which is counted higher
in the home above.

My Auntie Kate was a dressmaker, and very proud of the way she dressed me. When my Uncle Billy got married, she made my outfit as I was a little flower girl with white suede shoes and socks. My outfit was a white muslin frock with flounces and a mop cap. Kate starched my petticoat to make my frock stick out and she also starched the frills on my pants. As Annie, the little girl next door was going to the cantata at church with me, I went to call for her. She wasn't quite ready so Billy, her dad said, 'Sit down Molly and wait.' 'I can't,' I answered 'They've starched me britches.' He turned to Esther, his wife saying, 'Poor bairn, her backside will be sore when she gets home.' It was only the frills on my knickers that had been starched but Billy thought that Kate had starched everything.

FOUR

Esther and the wee folk

Annie's mother, Esther next door to us was from a farm in Donegal and she could tell a grand tale. She would have us kids mesmerised with stories about the 'wee folk'. These 'wee folk' back in Ireland lived at the bottom of gardens and dressed in the same colour green as the grass and had toadstools for their umbrellas. Every night farmers would leave bowls of buttermilk out for the wee folk to wash their shimmies in. We used to ask, 'Wouldn't their shimmies stink when they were washed in buttermilk?' 'Oh no, these were magic shimmies' Esther would reply.

I sometimes used to call for Annie to go to school in the mornings. Well, we'd had nowt to eat at Grandma's and at Annie's they'd all be sitting having streaky bacon and eggs. Billy would say, 'Esther, give Molly a bit of bread and some bacon dip.' Oh, it was good.

One day Esther was talking to Grandma about a local housekeeper called Liza. Esther was saying that Liza outshone us all with her black-leaded grate and how her brasses were beautiful. 'Well,' said Grandma 'I put a few drops of vinegar in my blacklead, that helps the shine but it still doesn't compare with Liza's'. Jimmy, Esther's three year old son was listening to this conversation and piped up, 'Liza tiddles in her blacklead' 'Oh', said Esther turning to Grandma, 'I didn't know about that. But I daren't do that in my blacklead because if it got hot and got to smelling, my Billy would create something terrible.'

FIVE

The Coronation and the Maypole

I can just remember King George the Fifth being crowned King. McIntyers from Cartgate Mansion gave us all a party. There were games and all sorts of things. I had a coat made out of teddy bear cloth that Aunt Kate had got as a remnant at the drapers shop at Cleator Moor. She also made me a hat with artificial cherries on the crown, a delphinium blue dress with a little round collar and cuffs, a yoke with feather stitching and a full skirt. I had little brown polished shoes and my grandma knitted me some honeycomb white socks and white gloves. I was so proud of these, you know. Us kiddies were given a cup with King George and Queen Mary printed on the side. And all the old folk got a cup, saucer and plate, with printed flags on them.

When I was older, there was Mayday. Keekle, Goosebutts and Galemire all joined together for that. Mrs Smith used to give us this 'do' from Galemire House and Bob Newall always used to lend us his donkey and trap for the May Queen to sit in. It's a funny thing, but there always used to be mayflowers, those little pink flowers, in them days. And we'd pick a bouquet of these for the May Queen and follow in the May procession. The maypole, at the top of Mrs Smith's big garden, was just like a telegraph pole but with hooks on it. From these hooks they used to fasten horse braids of every colour and us kids would hold the braid and dance round the maypole.

Mrs Smith always gave us a good tea on that day. Then Annie, her eldest daughter used to take us to the pictures at Cleator Moor. Well, we never used to go to the pictures and this was a treat. Annie would give us all a penny to put in the Nestle's slot machine to get a bar of chocolate before we went into the pictures. She would then seat us in the twopenny seats and after the film was finished, we would be regimented in a procession to the chip shop. Chips had been ordered for us, which we got, piping hot, in a triangular paper bag. The woman who had the chip shop used to ask us if we wanted salt and vinegar and she always gave us, what they called, crawklings, which were pieces of batter from the fish. We were never as well fed as we were that day. Well, what I've always wondered about since then, is why, after all we'd eaten all that day, and having chocolate and then chips and crawklings, we were never sick?

SIX

'Tha'll nivver larn'

Sometimes I was a naughty girl and Grandma would send me to bed until I said 'Sorry'. Now, below the windowsill in the bedroom was a shelf where all sorts was kept including the family bible. It was a big, green plush bible with a filigree cross in the centre and filigree round the edges. I could hardly lift the bible, so I used to kneel on the floor and turn over the pages and read the family details. There were all the births, deaths and marriages, of my grandmother's own grandmother's family at Maryport. I'd be so busy reading, I'd forget to say sorry for what I'd done wrong. Being sent upstairs and reading wasn't a punishment to me.

At nights, when there was only me and Grandma, we didn't close the curtains. We didn't light any paraffin lanterns either so the moonlight used to come streaming through the windows. The fire would be burning away, and Grandma would be sitting in her chair and I'd be sat on a copy (stool) at her feet, with my head on her knees. That's when she'd tell me all these folk stories and stories of our family long ago. She told me about the maids in service years ago who had porridge with treacle for their breakfast, tripe tatie-hash for their main meal and a scone at supper time.

Then there was Grandma's stories about her father, my Great-Grandfather Studholme. He was a lowland Scot from Ayrshire who married a neighbour's daughter at Gretna Green. Both families were scandalised and the girl was locked in her bedroom until the banns were read in the local church. The couple married but the girl died in childbirth. More up to date when Loweswater was frozen over there was skating and a feast with roast ox the side of the lake. Great-grandfather Studholme drove the horse and dray from the local brewery to the feast and that's where he met his second wife, my great grandmother who's folk tenanted Hopebeck Farm belonging to Squire Gaskell.

You know, I was an uneasy bairn and except for listening to Grandma's tales, I could never sit still. Especially if it was a wet day and I had to be 'a good lass' and sit and learn. I was taught to darn, using an oval tin covered with flannel, fastened on with elastic. I'd weave the

Great grandfather Studholme,
the Lowland Scot
who married at Gretna Green

needle in and out of the flannel and it had to be as neat at the back as on the front side. It was a disgrace to lend one's name to anything other than neat I was told. If my darning wasn't right, I had to unpick it and start again. I was taught to do corkwool on a wooden bobbin with four tacks in the top and odd pieces of wool were woven together and made into slippers with the aid of two pieces of shoe size cardboard. Old felt hats were stretched and steamed over a pan of water, cut shoe size and buttonholed over the cardboard.

At the age of seven I knitted my first jumper, brown with beige squares. I had to unravel the bottom because I hadn't woven the colours in properly at the back. 'What a bother' I thought. To get our wool, Grandma and me used to collect it in a basket from the barbed wire and hedgerows around the fields. The wool would be washed and teased up and I'd be sent to the chemist's to buy three penny-worth of logwood and copperace. These were mixed together with a cup of vinegar and two hands full of salt and put into this black dye. The wool was stirred into it and after it had been dyed, Grandma would spin it and put the wool into balls.

Talk about the terrible knitters of Dent, they had nothing on Grandma. She used to knit hug-me tights, which were knitted waist coats with bright buttons stitched on. She knit shoulder shawls, turn down stockings for our lads, and men's full length working stockings. Into the toes and heels of the stockings Grandma would put a bit of linen thread in the wool, so that they didn't always want mending.

I'll always remember the first pair of fully fashioned stockings that she knitted me. First of all, I had to collect all the fallen, dark brown oak leaves. These were simmered in a pan until brown dye ran out of them. In this mixture Grandma dyed some wool which was used to knit my first long stockings with a seam up the back of them.

I was taught to crochet and do shell-edging for pillowcases, petticoat bottoms and linen blinds. Next, I was shown how to embroider. I was sat on a chair and shown how to do these things. Child like, I used to wriggle to the edge of the chair when I'd had enough. Gran, a real Cumbrian would say, 'Man alive bairn, can't tha sit still a minute? You would think tha hed a clew o worsted up thee bottie.' A clew was the wooden bobbin on the spinning wheel. Then she'd continue, 'Stop thee hustling, sit still, tha'll nivver larn. Thou'll either be a useless numbskull or a ninnyhammer' So I tried to sit still and learn, more from the fear of being a numbskull than a desire to achieve anything useful.

Mind, I did play with other children when it wasn't too wet to 'humbug' other folk as Gran called it. When Aunt Kate had people to the house for their garment fittings, I went to play with May Smith at Galemire House and her mother fed me with the rest of the family. Mrs Musgrove from Galemire sometimes gave me tea with her grand-daughter, Mollie Wills who was my special friend.

SEVEN

Grandma's disabills

'Dear old Grannie in her 'disabills'
Molly and her Grandmother

Grandma's day started at five thirty a.m. when she put on her 'disabills' as she called her old working clothes. Every day the living room windows were cleaned by her 'so as not to loose any daylight'. When all the family were still living at home, Grandma used to have a baking day on a Tuesday and Friday. She baked half-a-stone of either wheat flour or brown flour.

From the Co-op at Cleator Moor I had to get three farthings' worth of yeast for every half-stone of flour to be used. If Grandma was making brown bread, she would add treacle to the flour and I had to take a jam jar to the Co-op where you got the jar full of treacle for a penny. The treacle was kept in a barrel which had a tap on the side. When the tap was turned on, out would run thin treacle. One kid who lived near us went to the Co-op for treacle and when they filled her jam jar and asked for the penny she said, 'It was in the bottom of the jam jar. Didn't you take it out?' She knew what she was doing!

After Grandma had added her treacle to the flour, in would go the yeast, a handful of salt, a spoonful of sugar and a dash of pepper. Then she mixed in either luke warm water or blown milk, which was skimmed milk with the cream taken off. When Grandma had worked it all together with her hands, she'd put the bowl on the floor, go down on her knees onto the mat and pummel the mixture. Finally, the mixture was put into warmed greased bread tins and the tops were always pricked all over with a fork. As she was doing that Grandma would say, 'A woman that sticketh her bread with a knife, isn't fit to be a wife.'

Carr's flour was two shillings and sixpence for a stone and we usually got five or ten stone bags. After using the flour, bags were bleached and made into pillowcases, or curtains which were dyed yellow with dolly tints. Even children's petticoats and bloomers came from the flour bags. All discarded clothes were washed, dyed and made into hearth rugs done on hessian, mostly sugar bags. A design was drawn on and prodded, then clippings of material, a finger length long were pushed through. Finer material was cut into longer lengths and knitted with string to strengthen them into bedroom mats, oval and long in shape. Stair carpet was also knitted.

Yes, Grandma was a marvellous 'thriver' as the saying was in those days. A make-doer, mender, knitter, sewer, and cleaner. Together we gathered herbs and wild fruits for puddings and crab apples for jelly. Wild damsons and sloes were for herbal remedies. We also got permission to gather fallen boughs in the plantations which Auntie sawed up for firewood.

Each night before going to bed, Grandma would get the oatmeal porridge ready for the next day. Lukewarm water went in with the porridge, a little salt and then she'd stir it all round with a pot stick before leaving it to swell overnight. You didn't get any frog spawn (lumps) in Grandma's porridge like some folk had in theirs.

EIGHT

Three red herrings and a barley loaf

At Christmas the cottage was always decorated with berry holly and we had a Christmas cake, mince pies and plum pudding. When Grandma was mixing the plum pudding mixture, a new sixpence in a larl bit of paper was put it. On Christmas Day, I always had the sixpence in my piece of pudding. As a rule I'd have a stocking filled with an orange, apple and some toffees. By that time, Auntie Sally and Uncle Billy were working so they would buy me something nice. Once Aunt Sally bought me a German doll, a china one but it wasn't for playing with just for looking at.

We used to 'Jolly Boy' at Easter. Us kiddies used to black our faces, put on an old feller's hat, wear a pair of old men's trousers, carry a walking stick and make a moustache out of soot. Then we'd go round the houses and folk would give us dyed pasche eggs. That was Jolly Boying. Besides going round the houses, we called at the Ewe Lamb pub at Pardstow. Jane, the landlady wouldn't let us go into the bar but the fellers used to come outside, look at our costumes and give us some pennies. Jane and her husband always gave us pasche eggs and an orange. Nobody else EVER gave us an orange. Well, this particular time, an old tin miner from Cornwall, who'd come up this way to work in the ore mines said, 'Which one of you is going to sing for us?' So I sang a dirty song. I don't know why I did, it was one of those type you sing in the school yard when you think no-one can hear you. Even now I blush when I think of it.

As kids we used to go round mumming, singing carols. We used to take a little Dorothy bag with us, which was a little bag made out of material with a frill on and a little handle over. Usually when women crocheted they kept their crocheting cotton in one of these bags. Anyway, off we went carol singing and stood outside the Ewe and Lamb pub. Of course, fellers in the pub would give us pennies, half pennies and groats which were copper four penny pieces.

There was still the old traditions around. When anybody had a baby, neighbours and relations would come and see it and be given rum butter and cream crackers. These visitors would often bring a silver threepenny bit and try to put the money in the baby's hand. You see, if the baby grabbed hold of the money and held it tightly, folk would say, 'That one's going to be a grabber' - you know, hold on to money. All these silver threepenny pieces would be put into a jar and eventually there would be quite an accumulation.

Now, when a couple got married, kids would fasten the church gates up with rope. They wouldn't let the couple out until they'd thrown coppers at the kids to pick up. The kiddies used to scrabble to see who could get most coppers. But if the couple didn't throw money, the kids would shout, 'Scrobey wedding, three red herrings and a barley loaf' Scrobey meant you were mean.

Most folk - grown ups and kids - had only one set of good clothes that they wore on Sundays when they went to church. Before Sunday, the clothes were always sponged and pressed, then put on the line to be aired. After the clothes had been worn, they were put away in a tea chest on the top of the stairs until the next Sunday or whenever they needed respectable clothes for weddings or funerals.

At funerals in country districts, they didn't have hearses or coaches, what they had was a brier. This was a long plank of wood with two handles on the side, resting on four wheels. The coffin was placed on the brier and four fellers used to push it while all the mourners walked behind.

I always remember when an Irish man my granda used to work with died. Granda had always talked about his mate saying, 'He's such a smashing feller and he's got such a grand family' Well, when this chap died, Granda got washed and changed and went to pay his respects to the family. When Granda arrived at his mate's house, the family and friends were having a wake. They had washed and put a fresh night shirt on the body and there he was, stuck in a corner. The men folk were drinking whisky, there were violins playing and folk were singing, 'Oh, Connell, Connell why did you die and leave us all to wail and cry' and all that carry on. It did upset Granda because he'd never been to an Irish wake before.

NINE

There was a King in Germany

I was four when I started Keekle Terrace School. I'll tell you what my Grandma used to do before I went to school, especially if any of her other grandchildren were staying with her. She used to regiment us in front of her to see that our footwear was properly cleaned. She used to see that our ears were clean, and we'd washed behind them and to see that we'd washed our neck. Oh, you were fed up before you got through the front door.

At Keekle Terrace School there were two classrooms and three teachers. Granda's cousin, Sally Calder, was the infant school teacher. We all used to have a tray of sand and Sally would draw things like simple addition or the alphabet on the blackboard and we used to copy them on the sand. Later on we had slates instead of sand trays to use. Once a year we'd have school prizes but during the First World War we got a certificate to show we'd been entitled to a prize. Our prizes or most likely their worth went for comforts to the soldiers.

Granda was a good royalist and he was born on the same day and year as Kaiser Bill. Once when royalty were visiting Lord Lonsdale they gave each of his employees a big coloured wall plaque made from Whitehaven clay on the Pottery Road. Eventually, this plaque was handed down to Granda and it was one of his prize possessions. But the day Kaiser Bill declared war on us, Granda was in a right state. 'Now Bill, don't be too hasty' said Grandma. 'You know that after his (Kaiser Bill's) father died, his mother gave him to Von Hindenburg and all he taught him to do was fight. You can't blame her and you can't blame Kaiser Bill.' Granda said, 'I'm going to get that sledgehammer and smash that wall plaque into the littlest bits I can and put it on the rubbish heap.' And he did!

At that time, we used to get the newspaper, the Sunday Pictorial as it was full of pictures about what was going on in the war. Granda used to go to the library at Cleator Moor to look at the shipping list and see where Uncle Harry's ship was. Uncle Harry was in the Merchant Navy

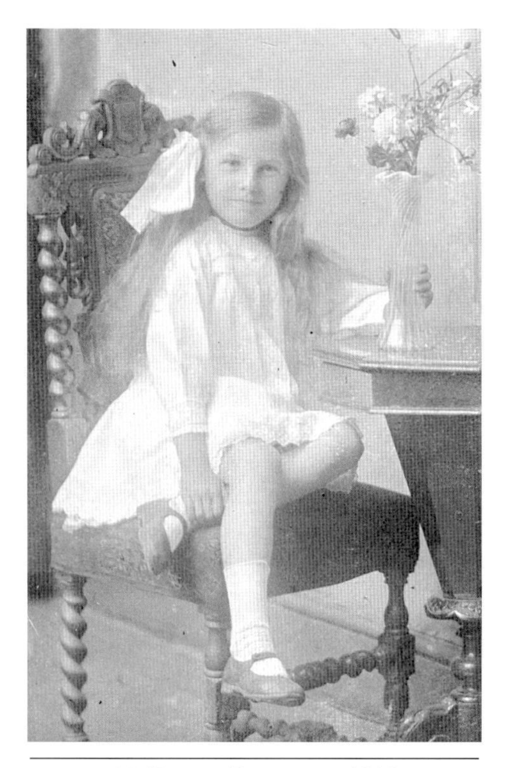

Molly age 7 years in 1915

during the First World War, and a lot of the captains made quite a bit of money bringing food over here from abroad. A cousin of Granda's who was a sea captain brought food over from Australia, the Cooke Islands and New Zealand. He 'run the gauntlet' as Granda said because he was flying the Argentinian flag, you see.

I can remember Uncle Tom, Granda's brother who had served seven years in India and was an army reservist. When he got his calling up papers for the Fifth Border Regiment and came to tell us he was going to war I was upset. I thought it was my Granda that was going to war and not Uncle Tom. Granda had died in 1916 and never saw Uncle Tom come safely through the war. The day Granda died, I wasn't told. I was sent to my mother's for the day and an auntie looked after all us kids while the other grown ups dealt with the funeral. After Granda was buried, Auntie Kate and me used to take flowers to his grave at the cemetery. We didn't have enough flowers in our garden to take, so I used to go to the back door of one of the mansions and buy flowers from them.

Nearly every other house at Hensingham and other hamlets lost a lad in the First World War. In August 1916, Uncle Tom and some other local lads were in a dugout on the Somme when it was bombed. They were all killed except Uncle Tom and another relation of ours. I know that when Uncle Tom came home, he told Grandma all about it. I heard him say, 'Being in India was bad enough, but in France, they were all the sons of folk we've known all our lives who were killed, and they were such nice lads.'

Another Uncle of mine, Uncle Bob was killed that day on the Somme. Uncle Tom took the bible out of Bob's pocket and brought it home. Before Bob was killed, like a lot of local lads, he'd done his training at Grantham Camp. While he was there, some bright spark wrote this song, which Uncle Bob sent to us.

There was a King in Germany, with half a dozen sons,
He raised a mighty army and filled his boats with guns
to pay a friendly visit to cousin George the King.
'Tis my royal intention, so come' said he, 'let's sing
It's a long way to Tipperary, it's a long way to go'.
Belgian cannons loudly said, 'You cannot come this way,
retreat at once or if you don't, we'll make you dearly pay'.
With zeppelins and aeroplanes he made a fierce attack
on Paris and her boulevards but he was driven back.
Bold Joffrey and his merry men are causing Bill to stamp
But he will swear the limit when he meets the lads from Grantham Camp.

Oh, during the First World War we had horrible margarine and couldn't have any sugar in our tea. If you did have sugar in your tea, you couldn't have any gingerbread or cake as there wasn't enough for both. Flour was black, what we used to call Russian flour. It was a terrible time though, because you knew everybody locally and they were all getting telegrams to say their lads had been killed. And the ones that came home on leave were hungry and lousy. They used to run lighted matches up their uniform seams to kill the lice.

There was a chap called John Travis Corwall who'd been killed in the Battle of Jutland and got the Victoria Cross. Stamps were issued to sell for the John Wallis Memorial Fund. Molly Wills, May Smith and me walked to Hensingham village to sell some of these stamps. We had a little bag with us that was full of pennies when we'd sold the stamps. Then it was time to go home but it was dark and we were afraid to walk through the plantations. I went and asked the village constable, Mr Irwin to take us home. Though I was the oldest child, I was also the smallest, so Mr Irwin carried me on his shoulders, giving me his helmet to carry for him. I never lived that down from Mollie and May. 'You were older than us but because you were the 'wee one', you were carried. We had to walk through all the mud'.

At the end of the war, you took your flags to school and had a party of sandwiches and drinks. But apart from that, there wasn't any street parties. There was too much poverty to have parties and also, with losing so many lads people weren't in party mood.

TEN

Spring physiking

When the First World War was over, it was terrible. People were dying with flu faster than they could bury them in hamlets and villages around.

Grandma sent me to help my dad as he was the only one in the house who didn't have the flu and he was looking after everybody else. I would be about ten or eleven years old at the time and was put to baking bread. I had to get down on my hands and knees on the mat and knead this bread in a bowl. I made eight loaves. Dad had been across at his garden and brought back carrots, turnips, onions and taties. We had some neck of mutton and made a big tatie pot in a great big roasting tin. But there was only Dad and me to eat it all as nobody wanted owt to eat, they were too ill. Then I came down with flu and Grandma 'physiked' me.

Grandma always talked about 'physiking you'. Anyway when I had the flu, she physiked me with caster oil and orange juice. Horrible. She used to do what was called 'Spring physiking'. Grandma had what was called a bread mug made of meadow pottery, brown on the outside and cream on the inside. Into this mug she used to put Epsom salts, lemons, and cream of tartar. I'd be sent to the chemist at Cleator Moor to get some black spanish (liquorice), that was as hard as a rock and Grandma would break it all up, pounding it with a flat iron. The spanish, along with treacle and sulphur was put into the bread jug with the other ingredients and it was all stirred round with a pot stick. In a morning before I went to school, I'd be given a small cup full. If any of our lot from Kells were staying, they had to have some as well. Our George, my brother, once said to me, 'Molly, it's a wonder we didn't shit ourselves before we got to school.' And you daren't cough anywhere near Grandma because she would dose you with hot milk and treacle, which I hated. When Granda was alive and had a bad back, she would fold a sheet of brown paper, put it on his back, then get a flat iron and iron it. Poor Granda.

ELEVEN

Auntie Fanny and the French side

By the early 1920's, there was only Grandma, Auntie Kate who was unmarried and me living together. Granda died in 1915; Uncle Billy married; Aunt Ginny was working away; and Auntie Sally was a governess at Southport. Auntie Kate was a dressmaker and tailoress. She could make men's suites as well as women's costumes. But money was scarce and though Kate could get heaps of sewing, she couldn't get the money for it. People still wanted finery but they couldn't pay for it. So she used to go sewing on the farms, staying away for a week. After the week Kate would land back in a trap with the farmer and she'd have potatoes, savoy cabbage or cow cabbage as we called it, eggs, boiling fowl and rabbit. If the farmers had butched a pig, they used to give Kate the spare rib, some sausage and blackpudding. In fact, she got a bit of everything because farmers never paid in cash, they always paid in kind.

When times got really bad and we were terribly hungry, Kate and me went to the French side of the family because they always had a good table and used to feed all and sundry. The French side was my dad's mother's side of the family. They came from France in 1762 and their name was Le-goffe but eventually it got changed to Goffet. Oh, we used to have such good meals with Auntie Fanny, my dad's sister.

Being brought up by a Quaker mother Aunt Fanny always had enough and some to spare for anyone dropping in. It didn't matter who came, Aunt Fanny would say, 'Sit down, there's plenty for everybody.' She had a long kitchen table, with two forms for everybody to sit on. When we were all sat down, she'd go to the oven, bring out the food and put it on the middle of the table and there was plenty for everybody. You weren't stinted.

For baking, Aunt had a two big ovens, one above the other. Puddings would be shut into the slow oven, then in the one on top there'd be a pie or roast beef and various vegetables cooking at the same time. I'll tell you what I used to like that she made. Steak and onion steamed pudding made in a great big enamelled basin. A three legged pan was put on the

Great Grandma & Great Grandfather Goffet, the business people at Whitehaven. C,1850.

jack and once it was boiling, kept it topped up with boiling water. That pie was smashing. And I often wondered what Auntie put in her mutton pie, which she served with onion sauce. I knew there was a leg of mutton, taties, chopped up onions and rosemary fastened up in a bit of muslin. That was good.

In them days, there were no cars to contaminate the countryside, so Aunt Fanny would use dandelions and young nettles for cooking with. She'd wash and chop them up, then add them to parsnips, carrots, turnips, leeks, split peas, ordinary peas, beans and everything you can imagine for a good soup. These would cook in water and savoury dumplings were added later on.

Another thing I used to like was Aunt Fanny's roast ham. Into the boiler would go a ham with cloves stuck into it and a pint of porter. When the ham was partly cooked, Aunt Fanny would take it out of the boiler, skin it, add brown sugar to the juices and pour that all over the ham, then finish it off in the oven. Once when me and Kate had been for our dinner, Kate said, 'Fanny Walker is a good cook, isn't she - or else we're so blooming hungry we appreciate her cooking.'

The French side of the family, after they came from France in the eighteen century, eventually settled at Whitehaven. They had a carrier business and had contracts for carting coal from the collieries to the railway stations. They got their horses from Stowe-in-the-Wold and Ireland. When they went across to Ireland for horses, they brought back a lot of Irish labour to work for them.

By the time of my dad's grandparents and parents in the last century, the family had land in Whitehaven, including Goffet's Yard. That was a bit of land bought for stabling horses and dad's mother had forty breeding sows there which she and her daughter Sarah looked after. Bacon pigs were sent to Liverpool and Manchester to a firm of bacon curers. Ordinary pork pigs were sold to local butchers, going as far as Egremont or Cleator Moor. My dad was only twelve years old when he used to put the pigs in a cart with a rope net over so they wouldn't fall out and take them to Cleator Moor. When his mother's elder grandchildren came along, they went to Nixon's private school on Inkerman Terrace at Whitehaven. But she still used to boil up the pig swill and these cousins had to go and feed the pigs so they wouldn't get above themselves.

Grandma Taylor. Daughter of great grandparents Goffet and mother of Molly's father. Photo taken at 'the Piggeries', Goffet's Yard, Whitehaven.

TWELVE

Everybody was struggling

From the end of the First World War until really the start of the second war, things were very, very bad for everybody. It didn't matter who they were. There were soup kitchens on Mill Street for school children where they could take their mug at dinner time and get a right, thick slice of bread and a mug of pea soup. It was always pea soup!

There were also soup kitchens for old people and the Work House was on New Road. Any widows or widowers who had no children to look after them, they had to go to the workhouse. Or any girls who had babies and weren't married. That was if their relations wouldn't have them as it was so shameful in those days. It was a dreadful thing, no matter if you were rich or poor to have a baby before being married.

I was getting bigger and growing older. Grandma was on parish relief because Kate wasn't getting any money for her sewing, you see. So I used to get time out of school to go into Whitehaven and collect this money. I'd be standing among a lot of old women with clogs on and shawls wrapped round them and there wouldn't be another kid amongst them but me. We queued up the Union Hall up Scotch Street to be given parish relief of five shillings a week. My dad and Uncle Billy each gave Grandma five shillings, so she had fifteen shillings a week to live on.

We were all right when Kate could get money for her sewing. But even at one of the mansions, where they used to get Kate to make uniform for their seven maids, believe me, she had a devil of a job to get her money from them. As a matter of fact, when one daughter from a mansion got married, she had a big marquee put up for the wedding and all sorts and Kate made a lot of clothes for the family. But they never paid and never paid so when I was going into Whitehaven to collect the parish relief, Kate wrote a letter to the husband of this girl who got married. He was a professional man and had an office in Whitehaven.

I went to the man's office and asked the receptionist if I could see him. 'Is it urgent?' she wanted to know and I told her that I had a letter for him and had to wait for an answer. Well, the receptionist gave the letter to this chap, who took me to one side and said, 'Have you got anywhere to put any money?' 'Oh yes,' I answered, 'I've got a bag here with a strap on underneath my frock.' So he put the money into an envelope, gave it to me and said, 'Just tell your Auntie that I'm very, very sorry about this affair. I didn't know anything about it.' He paid Kate in full.

But people were struggling at that time - everybody was struggling. That's why so many mansions went to the wall. All of them are gone now. The Bennetts from Whelpside mansion, they were good people. They used to go round all the old folk and take stuff for them. There was plenty of hand-outs from them if people were sick. Mrs Blair at Richmond Hill, she was quite kind. But others weren't and some of them were toffee nosed.

As Kate couldn't get her money things were desperate. For our breakfast we'd have a bit of dry bread and jam. And I'd also take dry bread and jam sandwiches to school with me. For our dinner at night, we'd just get a two and a half penny pork pie from the butcher and a quarter pound of potted meat and one boiled egg. That was between the three of us. Eventually Grandma said, 'I think you'd better go home, luv. It's the saddest day of my life that you've to go but if things get too bad, there's always a roof for you here. Don't expect a lot when you get home because the brood that Mary and Jack have fetched up themselves, will get preference to you every time. They won't have the same nature for you. Folk talk about adopted children and children brought up by other people, but unless they live on their own parents' doorstep, their mother and father don't know nowt about them.'

THIRTEEN

Living at Kells

Molly's parents. Photo taken at Whitehaven

Off I went to live with my mother, father, brother and sisters who were now living at Kells. There wasn't Woodhouse or Mirehouse council houses then, just Kells and that belonged to the colliery company. There was North Row, South Row, East Row, West Street and Mint Street and a sub post office, grocers shop and a miners welfare centre. That's all there was. The Yellow Earl, Lord Lonsdale had built these two-up and two-down houses. These houses hadn't ovens, so people used to cook everything over the fire. Then Lord Lonsdale built a big oven on Duke Street where miners families used to take their own loaves to be baked. Everybody used to put their own individual marks on the bread to make sure they got their own loaves back!

Do you know, when I went to Kells, they had such a good table. For their breakfast it was porridge to start off with or what they called Sunny Jim Force, which was like cornflakes. That was followed by bacon and eggs or poached eggs. Then when you came home from school at dinner time, there always used to be fish or meat and dumplings with two vegetables.

The Sugar Tongue at Whitehaven
(Courtsey of the Beacon Heritage Centre, Whitehaven)

When trawlers brought in their fish to Whitehaven and there was a glut it was auctioned to get rid of it. A chap with a hand-bell would come round the district shouting that there was a glut of fish on the Sugar Tongue at the harbour. So Dad would go down with his bass bag that had a few washed ferns in the bottom to keep the fish fresh. No women would go down to the harbour, only men went when the fish was all auctioned. Then Dad would come home with a whole cod or forty herrings for a bob, which was a shilling.

We used to have potted herring, which had been soused in vinegar, water, and salt and pepper. We would have these cold with a salad. Mother would stuff mackerel with bread crumbs, sage and onion, thyme and marjoram and a bit of suet. When there was new taties in the garden, we'd have new taties and peas with them. Gorgeous. If Mother got a whole cod, she'd cook the cod steaks and have egg and parsley sauce with them. The tail end of the cod would be battered and fried with chips. Then she'd wash the cod heads and boil them in an old pan, for the neighbour's cat. She didn't believe in wasting anything, didn't Mother.

FOURTEEN

An old Irish sea captain

At Whitehaven Mr Marzillier and Mr Shon didn't arrive there until the beginning of the Second World War. At first they made fire-lighters in the old town and what a stink they created with it. Later on they started Marchon Chemical works at Barrowmouth. Now, before they came, Barrowmouth was a beautiful place and we enjoyed going down there and picnicking on the red sandstone boulders.

At the head of the sea cliffs at Barrowmouth, lived Mr Greaves, an old Irish sea captain, in a cottage called Fort Hamilton. He had whale jaw bones for garden gate posts, kept hens and goats and had an Airedale dog for company. When Mrs Greaves had been alive, she was friendly with Grandma and Dad was friendly with their son, Billy who worked at Newcastle upon Tyne.

There was a spring at Barrowmouth where Mr Greaves got his water from by way of some spouting kept there. If anybody went there that he didn't like, he would pull the spouting away so they couldn't get a drink. But we could always get as much spring water as we liked. When we were going on a picnic to Barrowmouth, Mother used to bake him some gingerbread and currant and apple pasty. So off we'd go to Barrowmouth with a big picnic basket and a tin kettle. We'd gather twigs and brushwood and Dad would light the fire to boil the kettle and brew some tea. Then we'd go and see old Jimmy as we called him and take him some of Mother's cooking. In return Old Jimmy used to milk his goats and give us some of their milk.

With being a retired sea captain, old Jimmy was a whisky drinker but was never drunk. One day, I was playing down at Barrowmouth with my brother George when old Jimmy gave us this empty whisky bottle full of goat's milk. On the way home we sat down in a hedge and had a smell of the bottle. Even though it was full of goat's milk, it still smelt of whisky, so we had a taste. Well, we supped the lot and went to sleep.

When we eventually woke up and went home, Mother said, 'You've been an awful long time, I was beginning to worry and Dad was coming to look for you.' 'We drank this goat's milk out of a whisky bottle and fell asleep' I told her. Mother smelt the bottle and said, 'It's enough to make you drunk just smelling now and there's nowt in it.'

On the way to Barrowmouth was a huge black hut where women and children evacuees stayed during the First World War. I know at least one was French but the others were from Belgium. They were always very proud to think that King Albert of the Belgians was the only monarch to go into battle against the Germans in the First World War. We got friendly with some of the young Belgian girls and kept in touch with one called Maggie after the war when she went back home. Years later, after the Second World War, Maggie came back to this country for a holiday and came to look us all up. Well, there was a group of retired miners who were standing outside Nelly Smith's shop on East Row gossiping. She went up to them and one old feller just looked at her and said, 'Ah know thee. It's larl Maggie Seret, isn't it?" Maggie was a grown woman with five children by that time.'

Besides Barrowmouth, there was Fleswick Beach and Saltom Beach. I'll always remember, as a child and still living with Grandma, I went home to see my mam and dad. But they'd gone with the kids to St Bees on a Sunday school trip. Well, I got an old bucket, met a whole lot of kids that I knew and we went to Saltom Beach and picked cuvvins. Then we all went back to my parents house who like everybody else, didn't lock their doors. I went inside and as the fire was backed up, put the bucket of cuvvins filled with fresh water on the jack and cooked them. When the rest of the family came back these kids and me were all sat on our back-door steps eating these cuvvins with a pin. My dad asked, 'Where did you get those cuvvins?' 'Saltom Beach' I said, 'We went down there and gathered them.' Dad took the bucket of cuvvins which was still half full off us, saying 'You DIRTY little faggot. It's the sewerage bed on there. You'll all die of food poisoning if you eat any more of them.' He carried the bucket and tipped all the cuvvins into the quarry pond. Well, I've lived until I'm ninety so I didn't die of food poisoning.

The one event we were never allowed to go anywhere near was when there was the Orangemen's parade. That's when the Orangemen used to be marching along, playing tin whistles and singing songs encouraging the Catholics to retaliate. It was the same on Shamrock Day on the seventeenth of March, when the Catholics were marching. We would have got skinned alive if my father ever thought we were anywhere near those parades.

FIFTEEN

I'd rather have it out of a tin

Molly shortly after having scarlet fever

I'd rather have it out of a tin

I hadn't been home long at Kells when I had scarlet fever and had to go to the isolation hospital at Bransty. I had a cousin called Mary who had scarlet fever at the same time, so we were in the same ward. I can remember we were the only two kids in the ward which was emulsioned green. My mother and Auntie Kate used to come to the hospital door and leave things for Mary and me because they weren't allowed in. Then when Mary's mother came, she used to bring for us both. Somebody left us an orange each so there was Mary and me playing ball with these two oranges and throwing them against the ward wall. Matron was cross with us. The rest of the staff were all right. They used to rub us down with eucalyptus oil when our skin started peeling.

When I came out of the isolation hospital, my Aunt Sally took me with her to Southport, where she was a governess. It was a very big house where she worked and the owner, Mr Kearton, was a mill owner and had five mills. He and his wife had given Aunt Sally permission for me to stay there for a month while they went to Canada. When the Keartons came back from Canada, they rented a cottage at Cartmel so they brought me north with them in their duck egg blue Rolls Royce. Mr Kearton dropped the family off at Cartmel and drove me to Goosebutts. He brought Grandma an eleven pound salmon that he'd caught. She cut the salmon up into steaks and we took them all round the neighbours keeping one for ourselves. The remaining steak was cooked in vinegar and water and after eating it, Grandma said, 'I'll tell you what, it's was a big 'un but I'd rather have it out of a tin.' She didn't reckon much to fresh salmon!

SIXTEEN

A pillowcase full of washing

Back home, Mother got me a job sorting out the dirty washing at Whitehaven Steam Laundry, next to the Whitehaven cemetery. Business folk up Inkerman and Foxhouses Road would send their washing to the laundry. Pensioners got a cheap rate of one shilling for sending a pillowcase full of washing there. The laundry also used to do the washing for hotels and St Bee's School where lads were nearly all borders.

I used to start work at the laundry at eight o'clock and finished at six at night. You worked on a Saturday and got a good wage, which is what my mother wanted. Oh, I didn't like sorting dirty washing and was put onto the calenders. That was putting wet sheets through machines, putting red hot blankets onto pulleys, folding hot sheets or working on the presses. Your fingers used to get red raw with the steam.

After two years at the laundry I was sent to serve my time as a dressmaker. Mother got me into this place on Irish Street where a woman had eight apprentice dressmakers. Well, one after another, they left as they'd served their time. Eventually, after three months, I was the only one left. You see, Mother hadn't realised that the woman who run the place was closing down. This woman's husband was a Cornish sail maker and they were both going back to St Ives. So all I was doing was packing up and scrubbing out and paid five bob a fortnight for doing it.

Next, Mother found out that a doctor wanted an extra maid so she sent me to his house in Scotch Street. This doctor and his wife had a cook general, a parlour maid and I was the GBA - the general buggerer about. I lived in there, two of us slept in a room. It wasn't bad really and we had a good cook. My wage was five shillings a week. I started work at half past six in the morning, prepared vegetables, washed up after the cook and scrubbed floors. They had any amount of cats and had sand trays in the back kitchen for them. I had to wash these trays out, then put fresh sand in. Oh, the blooming spot stank with these cats.

If the doctor and his wife didn't have a dinner party, we would finish at about half past six at night. If they did have a dinner party, it would be a starter, then soup, the main course was something like roast beef or fowl. That was followed by a sweet, cheese and biscuits and coffee. The parlour maid and me used to help the cook to wash up but she would wash the pans herself.

SEVENTEEN

Whose lad ist thou?

I didn't have many friends because I still went to my Grandma's every weekend and took her parish relief. The only time I didn't go back was when I was working on a Saturday and then another sister would

'A wonderful Dad'. Molly's father.

take it. I used to go to a bible class through the week with one of my sisters. I remember two lads came to our house asking if we'd go to a social evening with them in the church rooms. Dad answered the door and when the lads asked him if we could go to the church rooms, he gave each them a right quizzing. 'Who's lad art thou? Does't thee father know yer here? Is thee servin' tha time? Ah weel, cum back when tha's finished thee time and tha can tek me lass out if ah think fit" Dad wouldn't let either of us go out and we were sixteen. And it was only to a church social.

We had a wonderful Dad. He was a miner and had worked at Wellington, Ladysmith and then was deputy overman at the Haigh Pit. Dad had lost an eye in a roof fall at the pit and when us kids were doing something we shouldn't, and saw him coming home, we'd take the dog out for a walk. We'd walk on the other side of the road, on the side of Dad's false eye hoping he couldn't see us. That was wishful thinking. Dad always said most women with families to keep were entitled to hold the purse strings. He gave my mother his pay packet unopened and neither smoked nor drank. What pocket money he had, he saved and took us to Eskdale agricultural show every year and for a ride on Larl Ratty. That was the highlight of our year.

In 1926, there was the General Strike when everybody was on strike, not just the miners. My dad didn't lose any work, he went to Jack, his pal who had a big farm at Wasdale and worked there and came home at the weekends. Every Saturday morning before Dad came home, I had to go to the colliery offices and pay the rent. One day, Mr Stephenson who took the money, said to me, 'Will you tell your dad to come and see me because every miner has been sent a pound from Mr Walker.' This Mr Walker was a colliery owner who was in Switzerland because he had TB. Anyway, I gave the message to my dad who said, 'He knows where he can put his pound. I've never had charity in my life and I'm not having it now.'

EIGHTEEN

'My wife is Madam'

I worked at the doctor's for nine months and then our mam would have me go to the Beehive, the department store on King Street. The wage was still five shillings and you wore your own clothes, a dark skirt and white blouse. I was in the office for a while doing things like accounting and then I moved onto toiletries counter. On toiletries, there was shampoos for washing hair, talcum powders and perfumes. One of those had such an overpowering smell, it was enough to knock you down. We also sold lipstick, eye-brow pencils and all the rest of it. Mind, it was only the middle class who had plenty of money for things like that. Ordinary girls didn't wear any make-up, they had a good wash instead!!

I was only at the Beehive for about nine months when a cousin who was working at Ainsley Top near Huddersfield as a cook housekeeper came home on holiday. She mentioned to my mother that she knew of some people at Huddersfield who were looking for a maid and did my mother know of anybody.

Off I went to Huddersfield on the train. From Huddersfield I got the tram so far then walked the rest of the way carrying my big case. The place where I went to was an old country mansion, with a great big stone wall around it. The man of the house greeted me with, 'Don't speak unless you're spoken to. My wife is 'Madam' and I'm 'Sir'.

The house consisted of a kitchen, back kitchen, dining room, drawing room and morning room. I should think there was five or six bedrooms and a bathroom upstairs but I was never allowed up there. I used the back stairs to go to my room. My bedroom was beautifully furnished with a nice bedspread and chintz curtains but I cried myself to sleep many a night. I hated working there and many a day I had no-one to speak to.

I was the only maid and the owners didn't have any more staff. I started work at half past six in the mornings and wore a lavender gingham frock with a white apron and bib. In an afternoon, I changed into a black frock with a little white apron which had lace round it. Besides housework, I cooked at breakfast and tea time. If the couple had a dinner party, I sometimes wasn't in bed until midnight. However, they were out an awful lot in the evenings and I was in this big house on my own and I was terrified. I didn't really have time off and even worked on Christmas Day, having my dinner in the kitchen on my own.

The couple had a lot of friends who used to come in the evenings. One person who came was the actor Basil Rathbone, but the lady of the house was against him coming. She was snobbish about that, she didn't want any actors in her house. However, as her husband and Basil went to the same school together he ended up coming to the house and then going to the theatre and acting at night. Mr Rathbone left me a ticket to go to the theatre and the lady of the house took me there. So I went with her who'd objected to anybody on stage staying at her house. Afterwards he did well and went to America. He was a very nice man was Basil Rathbone.

My wage was supposed to be five shillings a week but as the lady was expecting a baby, she palmed the clothes she couldn't wear off onto me instead of wages. I wasn't well while I was working there. I started to puff up and came out in blisters so I went to a doctor who said it was emotional stress and told me to leave my job. While I was working my notice, the lady of the house got a girl from Wath-On-Dearne for me to train as a maid. Before the end of her first week, the girl turned to me and said, 'I'm not stopping here. I'm going home.' 'For the Lord's sake' I told her, 'let me out of here before you go home.' Fortunately she did and I came home.

NINETEEN

It tickled me pink

Molly in 1927 while working in Wales

Mr and Mrs Kearton in Southport who Auntie Sally worked for moved to Flintshire in North Wales. They wanted an in-between maid and I went there. The mansion they lived in stood in it's own grounds. They employed seven inside staff besides a chauffeur, a chauffeur handyman, head gardener, undergardener and two apprentice gardeners.

As in-between maid I helped the parlourmaid and did her job if she had a half-day off or was on holiday. When the kitchen maid was off I helped the cook, preparing vegetables, washing up and things like that. Sometimes, if the nursery nurse was off on her half-day, I'd bath the kids and put them to bed. You see, I just fitted in anywhere. I was run-about for everybody. I didn't mind, the staff were lovely and Mr and Mrs Kearton were very nice.

Some of the staff slept two to a room, sleeping in a single bed. Both Auntie and I had a bedroom each. For starting work in a morning, I wore a lavender Horrock's gingham frock, a big white pinny and a cap. In the afternoon I changed into a black frock, a short white apron and black shoes and stockings.

The cook used everything of the best for her cooking. There was mallard, teal, roast of beef, legs of lamb ... oh, everything and nothing spared. Whatever the owners got, you got. You all had the same to eat. The Kearton's did quite a bit of entertaining but any left-overs they had, it wasn't given to the cook and warmed up for us or made into soup like some places. The food was given to the chauffeur or chauffeur handyman for their families so they could eat everything while it was fresh. Everything was shared.

I remember the Friday breakfast. We all used to have orange juice and cereal with milk. After that we had kippers, which had been cured with oak chippings and were roast in front of the fire for us, followed by toast and coffee. Even on Christmas Day we all had exactly the same meal with vintage wine and champagne.

On Christmas morning, Mr Kearton played Father Christmas. All the staff were each given five pounds. That was quite a lot in those days because a farm labourer's wage was only a pound a week. All the female staff were given a string of pearls in a satin lined leather box. Auntie Sally's string of pearls were genuine ones, real cultured pearls.

My wage was five shillings a week and my keep. Auntie Sally got more of course and sent some of it to Grandma. Mrs Kearton was very good because she'd say to us both, 'Can you make use of anything of Mr Kearton's?' Any of the clothes he didn't want, we could send home to our Uncles or cousins. And it was real good stuff we were given.

The mansion was quite near the village of Northop. The Kearton's didn't insist we went to church but we all did. It was only about five minutes' walk down the main drive. It wasn't a chapel, Church of Wales I should think and there used to be social evenings in the church hall. Once there was a prettiest ankle competition. Us girls had to stand behind a screen and lift our frocks up so everyone could see our ankles. I was the winner and was given a present of a brace of rabbits and a hundred weight of taties. They were no good to me because we had everything at the mansion so I gave them to somebody I knew with a few kids. It tinkled me pink did that ankle show.

The Keartons used to take a lodge for shooting and fishing up at Ardgay in Scotland and take some staff with them but I never went. However, they'd sometimes go touring from their mansion. They had three cars, a Lanchester, a Rolls Royce and a Spanish car but for touring they'd only use two with the chauffeurs driving. Occasionally they'd take me with them. Mr and Mrs Kearton, Auntie as the governess and the eldest child sat in the front car. The rest of us, the other three kids and me were in the back one.

We went touring to places of interest such as Red Wharf Bay in Anglesey, the Vale of Clwyd, Eastbourne and up near Chester. We all had our meals together. The Keartons were just natural, normal, nice, kind folk and there was nowt uppity about the kids. They never treat you different. There wasn't any 'Yes Ma'm. No Ma'm'. And the rest of the staff weren't jealous about me going off. They were a lot older than me and never seemed to mind where I went. Oh, I did enjoy those days out.

Some of the staff at Glencalvie lodge, Ardgay. 1927

TWENTY

They all sat up in bed

I'd been working in Wales for nearly two years. By this time, my younger sister Blanche who was working as a probationer nurse at the County Hospital in Kendal started with rheumatic fever and had to go home. Now, nurses had to buy most of their own uniform in those days, so mother was left with this uniform. Lo and behold, the first thing I knew was, Mother was sending me in Blanche's place.

Molly at the Westmorland County Hospital, Kendal 1929

At the County Hospital, you were supplied with the dress but had to provide your own apron, cuffs, caps, collars, black shoes and black stockings. Of course, no jewellery was allowed. The first three months you had no pay, that was to see if you were satisfactory. You started at twenty-to-eight in the morning and had two hours off in the afternoon when you were supposed to swot. Then you were back on duty and worked until twenty to eight at night when the night staff came on.

We lived in at part of the hospital and got all our meals made by a good cook who used to spoil us to death. If we came in later than we should after an evening out, she would let us into the hospital through her quarters. Unfortunately the cook retired and the next one that came wasn't so good. She used to pickle eggs in chloroform and you used to get these when you went for your breakfast. When we were on nights, the chops that we were given were only half cooked.

Some of our patients when they were discharged used to land up to the side door of the hospital. One chap who had a big garden used to fetch us tomatoes, lettuce, spring onions and all mix of stuff. Another lad, who worked at the little grocer's shop up Beastbanks used to come to the side door after he finished work with chicken and some eggs. Us nurses would cook the chicken in the kitchen oven, then put disinfectant down the sink so that the Sister couldn't smell it when she was on her rounds. We used to have some right tuck in's.

As a probationer, you made beds, gave patients a bed bath, cleaned out their lockers, helped Sister when she was doing dressings, took the dirty ones away to the sluice and things like that. You washed patients every morning and combed their hair. When a patient died, along with somebody else, you laid them out. Somebody always died if a visitor brought a mixture of red and white flowers in to a ward. It was just one of those things that used to happen. As soon as anyone brought red and white flowers, you took the flowers away and divided them into just red flowers or white ones.

We also had some right good laughs. Once we had a men's ward full of men who were up and ready to go home. None of them were really poorly so the nurse who I was on duty with said, 'Let's get some red ink and dab all their noses while they're asleep.' If you'd seen them twitching while we did this but they didn't waken. When they all sat up in bed the next day and saw each other's noses, they started to laugh. Anyway, the night Sister sent us both to the Matron for insubordination. But Matron Connell was laughing when she heard about it and said, 'It's very unprofessional of you, you know but go on, get out of my sight.' Oh, Matron Connell was lovely. She was one of the nicest people you could ever have met.

After three months at the hospital, I had seven shillings and sixpence a week. To get your month's pay, you went to the Matron's office, where the Matron was at one side of the desk and the Sister tutor at the other. Once you got your wages, Sister tutor would want some money off you for the Aged Nurses' Fund, and then money to make things for the Parish Church Bazaar. When you got out of that room, you nearly had nowt left.

Once a year, there was Gala Day for the hospital, when there was a May Queen Procession. All the businesses in Kendal used to contribute to the Gala Day and at night, there was a dance at the Town Hall. Of course, everybody couldn't go from the hospital, so the Matron used to pick two of the staff to attend. It was really grand. When Paul Robeson, the American singer gave a charity concert in the Town Hall there were so many tickets allocated to the hospital. I went with Sister tutor and Matron and I enjoyed that show. Paul Robeson was really smashing.

The Westmorland General Hospital was a free hospital. That meant that patients didn't have to pay as the upkeep was made by donations from the people of Kendal. And all the doctors who had practices in the town gave their services free for a month every year. The ones who were surgeons, were on call day and night for operations.

I loved babies, so my favourite ward was the baby ward. I liked bathing and changing them. There was no washing machines in them days and as probationer nurses we had to wash the nappies in buckets in the sluice. As soon as babies had been born, we rubbed them all over with olive oil to take the slime off, then we bathed them. Every time you changed a baby's nappy, you bathed the baby and rubbed its bottom with olive oil. Then when they wet their nappies, the urine didn't penetrate onto their skin. We never had a baby leave the hospital with broken skin because of wet nappies. If the kiddies were a bit fractious and cried through the night, I'd warm a blanket, roll them up in it and love them until they were asleep. I was really happy at the hospital, really happy.

TWENTY ONE

Thou's a big lass, now

'Grandma died of cancer and the bottom dropped out of my world'

At the hospital we had the Parish Church curate come on a Sunday and take the service in alternative wards every week. If we didn't want to go to the service, we could be excused and I would catch the four o'clock bus to Whitehaven. That cost three shillings return but instead of going home to my mother at Kells, I'd walk past the forests and plantations to Grandma's house at Goosebutts. It was usually night time but that walk never bothered me.

Grandma and Auntie would be in bed and when I knocked on the door Grandma would come downstairs with a candle in her hand and say, 'Man alive bairn, I wouldn't have slept in my bed if I'd known thee was coming.' In I'd go and she'd make me some cocoa and something to eat. Then I'd get into my nightie and into bed. In the dark Grandma would say, 'Thou's a big lass now, thou would have only had a mile and half to walk to thee mother's.' 'I didn't want to go, I wanted to come home', I'd tell her. She'd answer, 'Well, I won't always be here and the sooner thou larns it the better.' Then Auntie would pipe up, 'As long as it's my home, it'll be her home. She'll always have a home to come to.' But shortly after, Grandma died of cancer and the bottom dropped out of my world.

TWENTY TWO

Love causes insanity

I was at the Westmorland Hospital for two and a half years and then I got myself married. This is what happened. I'd met Ted at the hospital but didn't go out with him then. One day I was going to Heversham on the bus and as it was packed Ted gave up his seat for me. When we got to Heversham he said, 'Do you want to come down home with me? If you do, I'll take you back to the hospital on my motorbike.' So I went to the farm and met his family and that was the start of my courtship with Ted.

When we decided to get married we went to Whitehaven to tell my mother. 'I've had the expense of three weddings in eighteen months' my mother said, 'I don't want to hear anything about yours'. I wouldn't marry Ted in a register office so we were married by special licence at Kendal Parish Church with two friends as witnesses. I just wore a blue frock and hat at my wedding. After the wedding was over we went to a friend's house on Beastbanks for our wedding reception.

By that time I was a staff nurse at the Westmorland Hospital and my wage was twelve shillings and six pence a week. There was no married nurses at that time so once you were married you couldn't stay on. I'd really enjoyed nursing but they say love causes insanity, don't they? My grandma used to say, 'Courting's one thing, marrying is another because you never know the devil until you live with him.' She was right.

Ted was working at his family farm and we lived in a tied cottage. His wage was one pound a week which was the going rate for a married man with a tied cottage and a farm lad got about eight pounds for a half year. The cottage we lived at was at Leasgill. Our water was from the guttering that ran into the waterbutts. All the cottages had dry petties, except the gentry as they had their own cesspool and water supply. The gentry also had their own generators for electricity, while we used paraffin lamps and calor candles as they were cheaper to buy than wax ones. Of course, we used to get perks that the ordinary farm workers didn't get. If Ted's folk killed a pig we used to get a bit of it and we had a big garden and grew our own potatoes and vegetables.

From Leasgill we moved to Flodder Hall at the Lythe Valley. Oh, that was lovely and we had such good views. Flodder Hall was a very big house, it even had a wine cellar. There was a big sitting room and dining room. Then you went down three steps into the kitchen, which had wash boilers in and an old fashioned fire place. We had our own water toilet and outside, there was our cesspool at the top of the orchard.

We had ten acres of orchard, with damsons, plums, apples and a walnut tree. When my mother came to visit she used to take the walnuts home, bottle them and make walnut ketchup for my dad. There was a big peat moss on the farm so the peat was cut out, stacked and when it was dried out we used that for fuel.

As farm manager, Ted's wage was two pounds and fifty shillings. Besides Ted there was two other farm men. There was no social life but we did have a man who used to come round from the Kendal Co-op. He would take our order and deliver what we needed. But farmers didn't pay for anything. They'd exchange butter and cheeses for groceries and things like that.

My husband was nicely spoken and could be quite charming. It was only when I started ailing that things went wrong. That was when I had my first son, John. I was at home and in labour for four days before the doctor tried to deliver the baby with forceps. The baby was wedged in my pelvic girdle and it was decided to send me to the Lancaster hospital. Ted phoned Doctor Craig at Kendal who sent the ambulance out for me right away and brought me to the County Hospital where I had a caesarean operation. At that time they were performing caesarean's in cities but not in small hospitals. I was only the third person at the County Hospital to have one. When the Parish Church curate came to take the hospital service he baptised John, my baby. I was too ill to see John who died a few days later. Dr Craig told me he was a beautiful baby.

From then on at the hospital, I was special and spoilt to death. It was my twenty fourth birthday while I was in the nurses' sick ward and Matron bought me a pink crepe-de-chine nightie. Sister Smallman gave me pink carnations and some of the doctors pooled together to buy me some white heather. I had flowers galore and everyone that I'd worked with came to have a peek at me when I was fit to see them. I was seven weeks in hospital with ruptured uterus muscles and the devil knows what else. Anyway, when I was X-rayed Dr Craig asked, 'Were you ever hungry as a child as you're not properly developed? You may have another baby sometime, there's no rush but you'll have to have a caesarean.'

After I went home to Flodder Hall, members of the Hospital Committee used to come and see me and they all always brought me a present. I only weighed six stones, three pounds and couldn't put on an ounce. I suppose it was no wonder as I used to feed the calves and chickens, fetch the coal, chop sticks and when the taps run dry, take two gallon buckets down to the well and cart water up for the animals.

TWENTY THREE

My second baby

We'd been at the Lythe Valley for about two years when Ted decided to tenant a farm of his own and we went to live at Little Asby. We had to take the sheep over at this farm at valuation and pay a tithe for them on the common land. Our farm house was quite nice but there was no water in it. Water for scrubbing floors and that type of thing came from a water butt. For drinking water, I carried two, two gallon buckets about a hundred and fifty yards onto the fell, where there was a spring.

It was a nice farm house with two sitting rooms that looked out onto the garden, and four good bedrooms. However, the granary was attached to the house and rats used to get into it. Even if you covered the grain over, these rats managed to gnaw their way to it. And in bad weather, we got the fell ponies coming into the granary. When it started snowing, these ponies used to lift the yard gate off it's hinges, come into the farm yard and even managed to open the granary door. One night I heard them in the yard and granary. I got dressed, took the dogs with me and chased the ponies back onto the fell. Ted slept through it all and the following morning he says to me, 'What happened to that damn yard gate?' 'What do you think?' I said, 'I was out through the night, taking the dogs with me and chasing the ponies back onto the fell."

Winter could be bad. Once we were snowed up from October until the end of April and an engine on the railway line was stuck up on high line for all that time. Even our hens were snowed in. Ted managed to cut a pathway to the hen house but the snow was so deep, you had to feed them through the hen-house window. When we managed to open the hen house, there was eggs galore. During all this time, once a month the snow plough cut it's way through to us and brought flour, lard and things like that. It was a rough time.

In 1934 I was expecting my second baby. I arranged to go to Whitehaven for the birth. However, the night before Tom was born I was mowing hay and working up in the barn until midnight. I remember coming down from the top of the barn by cart rope and my hands were all burnt. At about half past one in the morning, my waters broke. Ted got the car out and took me all the way to Whitehaven hospital where, fortunately, our family doctor was doing his rounds. They did another caesarean on me and I was in hospital for five weeks, then stayed at my mother's before going back to Asby.

Looking back, my life was all baking, washing, cooking and cleaning. When it was haytime, I used to help Ted in the fields. Four o'clock in the morning I'd get up and start work. The baby would be fast asleep in his cot and the farm lad still asleep in bed. After I'd worked in the fields, I'd come back home, light the fire, put the kettle on and make Ted and the farm lad a cup of tea and something to eat. We didn't have much to eat then until breakfast time when they'd done the milking. Then I'd turn out into the fields again, taking the baby with me in his pram. I'd ride the siderake, turn the swathers off and tether with old Dick, our horse when Ted was mowing. I even used to walk the sow to the boar two miles away, pushing my baby in the pram at the same time.

I wouldn't even have had a pram only I knew the policeman's wife at Ravenstonedale who'd been at school with me. After she'd finished with her pram, she passed it on to me. You see, they didn't give you money, didn't farmers. They expected you to live off the land then when you'd made your butter and collected your eggs, what was surplus, you exchanged for groceries. I never had any new clothes. I wore all my sister Sally's cast-offs and as she was taller than me, I had to take them all up. However my husband managed to go to the pictures with his mates or go and watch the wrestling matches at Morecambe.

I remember Ted went to Ravenstonedale show and left me with our young baby and the sow due to farrow. The sow had fourteen piglets and as she hadn't enough teats to feed them with I looked after some of them. I bored holes in a tea chest with a red hot poker to get a bottle teat through, put some straw into the chest and brought some piglets indoors. Then I put powdered glucose into a jug of milk, stirred with the hot poker and put the mixture into a bottle with a lamb teat on. I sat up that first night feeding piglets from the bottle and managed to keep them all alive. That sow was Ted's special pet but she went for him open mouthed when he returned. He'd neglected her in her hour of need. The trouble was Ted's heart wasn't in farming. Mechanically, he was a wizard but he'd been brought up to work on the land.

TWENTY FOUR

Going onto the Moss

We stayed at Asby for about two years and then moved down to Yealand Redmayne. That farm was another one that had no water and just a dry petty up the farm yard. But it had the most gorgeous views. Again, we didn't buy the farm with Ted being a tenant farmer. You paid rent but your stock was your own. Hardly anybody in those days owned a farm because most were part of the landed gentry estates. Once a year the gentry had a rent day when the tenant farmers went to pay their rents. They were given a ploughman's lunch of bread and cheese and a pint of beer by the lord of the manor.

Shortly after we moved to Yealand Redmayne, the people who run the sub post office at Yealand Conyers were giving it up. I asked Ted if he would mind if I took the sub post office on because it would be extra money - about twenty two shillings and six pence a week. That's how I started the sub post office at our farm house. Somebody from the head post office at Carnforth came and showed me what to do and what stock I needed. We bought weighing scales and Ted built a counter for me and it was fit up in our parlour. I also had a coin phonebox in the parlour as well but nearly everybody and their mothers would want to use it at nights when we were closed.

The postman delivered his letters to me at six in a morning and picked up other ones up from my post office. He used to have a drink of coffee with Ted and me and then I opened up the post office at nine o'clock.

I did quite a bit of trade and was open until half past six at night for six days a week. Mind, with running the post office, I had to do all my washing on a Sunday and there was still baking to do every night. So I would be working until after midnight many a night and be up before the postman came at six the next morning.

People also bought their insurance stamps from me and I received and sent telegrams as well. The Second World War had started by then and there was more telegrams than I liked coming in about local lads who'd been killed. Ted or the farm lad used to deliver these telegrams. I used to think it was terrible, your neighbours getting telegrams to say that their lads had been killed or young wives being informed it was their husbands.

Quite a few evacuees came to the area. Until the poor little beggars were placed, they had them in the school room and some folks would go and pick which ones they wanted. The two evacuees that I had were two tail-enders. Nobody wanted them. Poor little kids, because they were scruffy, nobody wanted them. Some folk in big houses wouldn't have any evacuees, it was the ordinary folk that took them in.

The two lads that I took in were brothers from Salford and their father was away over-seas in the war. Their elder brother and mother stayed down at Salford as he was at the Grammar School and she was working as a confectioner. She sometimes used to come at weekends and stay overnight at the farm. One night when the two lads were in bed their mother told me some dreadful tales about houses being bombed and people being killed in Salford. She said she hadn't wanted her two younger sons to see anything like that and that's why she sent them up here.

Anyway, these two lads settled in all right until Silverdale railway station and one of our fields were bombed. That night most of the villagers at Yealand got together when they thought the bombs were coming too near. They decided to go onto the moss which was low lying. Ted had gone to see all-in wrestling at Morecambe so there I was under the stairs with these two lads and my own son with all this bombing going on. One of the farmers came and knocked on the door. 'Molly,' he said, 'These bombs are getting too darned near so we're all going onto the moss. Leave Ted a note and come with us.' 'No, I'm not' I told him. 'Ted might not have a key in his pocket and won't be able to get in the house.'

When the evacuees' mother came the following weekend, they told her about the bombs at Barrow and Silverdale Station and the crater in our field. They finished by saying 'We were all terrified and sitting under the stairs.' Their mother said, 'Oh well, I think I'll take them home because I needn't leave them here to be bombed.' So off she took them back to Salford.

TWENTY FIVE

A job at the Post Office

Farming had been bad for a few years even before the war started. Some were going bankrupt or committing suicide as they couldn't cope. We were in a bad way on our farm and sold up. We didn't go bankrupt, as what was outstanding we paid off. Within nine months of selling up, subsidies came in and if we'd hung on until then we'd have been as well off as we'd been badly off.

Ted volunteered for the RAF and I went back to my mam and dad's with Tom to Whitehaven and got a job at the post office. However, the RAF didn't keep Ted long and sent him home because of his experience of farm work. So he lived at his mother's and went to work for the War Agricultural Committee, taking prisoners-of-war to work.

Besides Tom and me my elder sister, Sally who was a school teacher at Kells School lived at home with my mam and dad. I worked on the counter at Lowther Street Post Office at Whitehaven. Quite a lot of others worked there, including the telephonists upstairs. We shared a retiring room with them. I worked an eight hour day so my life was really just going to work and returning to my parents and Tom.

Tom and me lived off my wage. Ted kept his wage as he hoped to set up in business again. I never knew how much he earned and he never told me. My mother used to give me her coupons to send in my letters to Tom so that he never went short. We had more coupons that we wanted at Whitehaven as my mother still used to do her own baking and my brother George was a butcher so that helped.

Mind you, I still used to wear my sister's cast offs. A cousin of mine, Frances died and there was nobody who her clothes would fit except me. So my Auntie said, 'Come and see what you want.' I got two suites, some blouses, two pairs of new shoes and this dress I'm wearing now and another one. 'There's a sable coat, a hat to match and fur lined boots that belonged to Frances,' said Auntie 'You can have them as well, Molly'

'What me, Ted's wife? No fear, if anybody sees me in Kendal with

Molly (wearing glasses) working at the GPO telegraph room, Kendal

them clothes on, they'll say I'm on the make with some blokes.' I told Auntie. She blew her top saying, 'Well, the best thing for you to do is come back home if that's they way they think.' The clothes went to a friend of Frances' who was a school teacher. Some time later I was with a friend when we saw this girl wearing the sable coat, hat and boots. My friend turned to me and said, 'They must have damn good salaries at school to afford clothes like that!!'

Nine months later, Ted managed to get two rooms on Appleby Road in Kendal for us to live together. I managed to transfer from Whitehaven Post Office to the Kendal one, so back we came to Kendal. Ted had sold all our furniture except what would furnish the two rooms and we just had an open fire and two hobs to cook on.

There were thirty six of us working at the post office in Kendal. I was doing counter work and on telegrams. Others were telephonists and the postmen of course. On the counter, we worked on a rota and did shift work. The latest I finished would be nine o'clock at night. In a morning, it could be six o'clock start with half an hour for breakfast. I'd have made everything ready the night before but would dash home in that half hour. I'd give Tom his breakfast before he went to school and have a cup of tea myself. Then I'd work until one o'clock and be back at work for half past four until seven at night. Our earliest finish was half past four and for lunch, it was just a forty minute break.

My wage was two pounds, ten shillings and five pence for a forty eight hour week. If somebody was off sick, staff had to cover between them. The post office was open until eleven on a Sunday morning, so if you worked then and covered for others, you'd work a sixty hour week. Even though it was long hours you did have some laughs.

There was a registered letter locker at the post office where you put letters for callers and often when you opened it, a cockerel would jump out. You'd go into the sorting office and shout to the postmen, 'Hey, which of you fellers have left a cockerel in the locker?' It would always be the same country postman who'd answer, 'Oh, it was me, Molly. Mrs So-and-so gave me the cockerel. She couldn't kill it so she gave it to me and my wife has it to kill and pluck.' I'd ask, 'Won't you kill and pluck it?' His answer was, 'Will I bedamned. The wife can do it, she's getting it for nowt.' That was a regular occurrence. About once a month, there would be a boiling fowl in the locker. They were always alive and you had to clean the blooming locker out before you could put your registered letters in.

When I was at the post office, my brother George, the butcher, didn't want me to hunger. He'd bed some eggs in lard, wrap a bit of steak around the lard and send it express post and I'd get it the same day. Well, of course when I opened the darned thing at the post office, folk were all over me like fleas and what could you do? You gave them a bit of this and a bit of that.

There was a prisoner-of-war camp at Bela, at Milnthorpe. These prisoners would be put to work on land draining or on farms for haytime, harvesting, potato picking and stuff like that. Like a lot of other fellers, Ted was a foreman in charge of these prisoners. The foremen drove the wagons with prisoners in to where they were going to work and then would oversee them. Ted always took his overalls and worked along side these men as he said it encouraged them. When he first went to work with the prisoners they were Italian prisoners-of-war who were as Ted said, 'A lazy lot of buggers. They want prodding up their backsides to make them work, yet they're always smiling.'

TWENTY SIX

After the War

Molly, age 60 (1968) still at the GPO telegraph room, Kendal

After the war was over we managed to get a council house in Kendal. Then Ted went away down south where a friend said he could get him contract work. He never sent any money home so I worked all the ruddy overtime I could at the post office. Ted used to come home for a week's holiday every year and sometimes for a weekend, from Friday night until Sunday night. I would say to him, 'Let me come down south and I'll see if we can get anywhere to live'. He'd answer, 'There's no houses because people who came as evacuees have stayed on. You can't get a house for love nor money. Apart from that, if I didn't come here for a break, I wouldn't get one.'

I divorced my husband on our twenty fifth wedding anniversary. He had no sense of responsibility and an eye for other women. Maybe I was to blame for allowing him to get away with it. Ted always said he was hard up so I'd worked to keep my son since he was seven years old. In the first eleven years of marriage, I had forty-seven pounds and ten shillings from my husband. With that money I bought him a suit, overalls, a raincoat and shoes. I think my fault was that I'd been brought up by a loving old Gran and a spinster Aunt. I wasn't used to male company and didn't know how to handle a man at all. Tom, my son was my saving grace. Without him I wouldn't have wanted to live.

I continued working full time at the post office and was eventually there for twenty seven years. I didn't smoke or drink and was scrimping away but I managed. A friend of mine used to love going to second hand sales. So on a Wednesday night after I'd finished work she used to meet me and we'd go and look at all the furniture. If there was anything I needed, I'd give her the money and she'd put a bid in for it the next day. So that's how I got my furniture and I'm still using some of it now. My biggest regret is that I hadn't enough money to let Tom go to university when he finished at the Grammar School but there was no grants in those days.

Except during the Second World War, I'd always kept in touch with Margaret Serret, the Belgian evacuee from the First World War. In 1962 she invited me and my sister Sally to visit her at Liege. Margaret's husband Robert was a teacher at the Brussels University and during his summer holidays he took us all over. As well as Belgium, we went to Luxembourg, France and into Germany. However, Margaret wouldn't

'Friends since the First World War'
Molly (centre), sister Sally (right) visiting
Margaret (left) in 1962

go to Germany with us. She wouldn't go over the German frontier as she said it made her shiver. Maggie died a couple of years ago but I still write to her family. Her grandson is now the Belgian Ambassador in Paris.

Today, at ninety years old I live alone in a flat with wonderful views of the trees, fields, farm animals and the distant hills. These are the things I've been used to all my life. I knit, sew and crochet for charity and do all my own housework and keep myself fully occupied. I'm now a great-grandmother and have a happy family.

I know I've had a chip on my shoulder because of my upbringing but I don't think it was a mistake being brought up by Grandma. It was a mistake that I didn't live anywhere near my own parents. You see, usually if a Grandma took a child, the parents lived in the same street and the kiddie could see their mam and dad every day. And there was a difference between townies and country folk in them days. The townies thought they knew everything so us, from the country were 'country born, country bred, strong in't arm and thick in't head.' But even though I've had a struggle, I've coped. God's been good to me.

Molly with son, Tom, on her eightieth birthday